CW01213195

OXFORD
UNIVERSITY PRESS

Great Clarendon Street, Oxford, OX2 6DP,
United Kingdom

Oxford University Press is a department of the
University of Oxford. It furthers the University's
objective of excellence in research, scholarship,
and education by publishing worldwide. Oxford is
a registered trade mark of Oxford University Press in
the UK and in certain other countries

Text © Oxford University Press 2024

Illustrations © Anastasia Yustus 2024

The moral rights of the author have been asserted

First Edition published in 2024

All rights reserved. No part of this publication may
be reproduced, stored in a retrieval system, or
transmitted, in any form or by any means, without
the prior permission in writing of Oxford University
Press, or as expressly permitted by law, by licence
or under terms agreed with the appropriate
reprographics rights organization. Enquiries
concerning reproduction outside the scope of the
above should be sent to the Rights Department,
Oxford University Press, at the address above.

You must not circulate this work in any other form
and you must impose this same condition on any
acquirer

British Library Cataloguing in Publication Data

Data available

ISBN: 978-1-382-04370-0

10 9 8 7 6 5 4 3 2 1

The manufacturing process conforms to the
environmental regulations of the country of origin.

Printed in China by Golden Cup.

Acknowledgements

Tala and the Lake of Secrets and *Tala's Lesson* written
by Giles Clare

Content on page 9, 29, 43, 61, 77, 86, 88 and 92
written by Suzy Ditchburn

Illustrated by Anastasia Yustus

Author photo courtesy of Giles Clare

Every effort has been made to contact copyright
holders of material reproduced in this book. Any
omissions will be rectified in subsequent printings if
notice is given to the publisher.

MIX
Paper | Supporting
responsible forestry
FSC™ C110497

Tala and the Lake of Secrets

Written by Giles Clare
Illustrated by Anastasia Yustus

OXFORD
UNIVERSITY PRESS

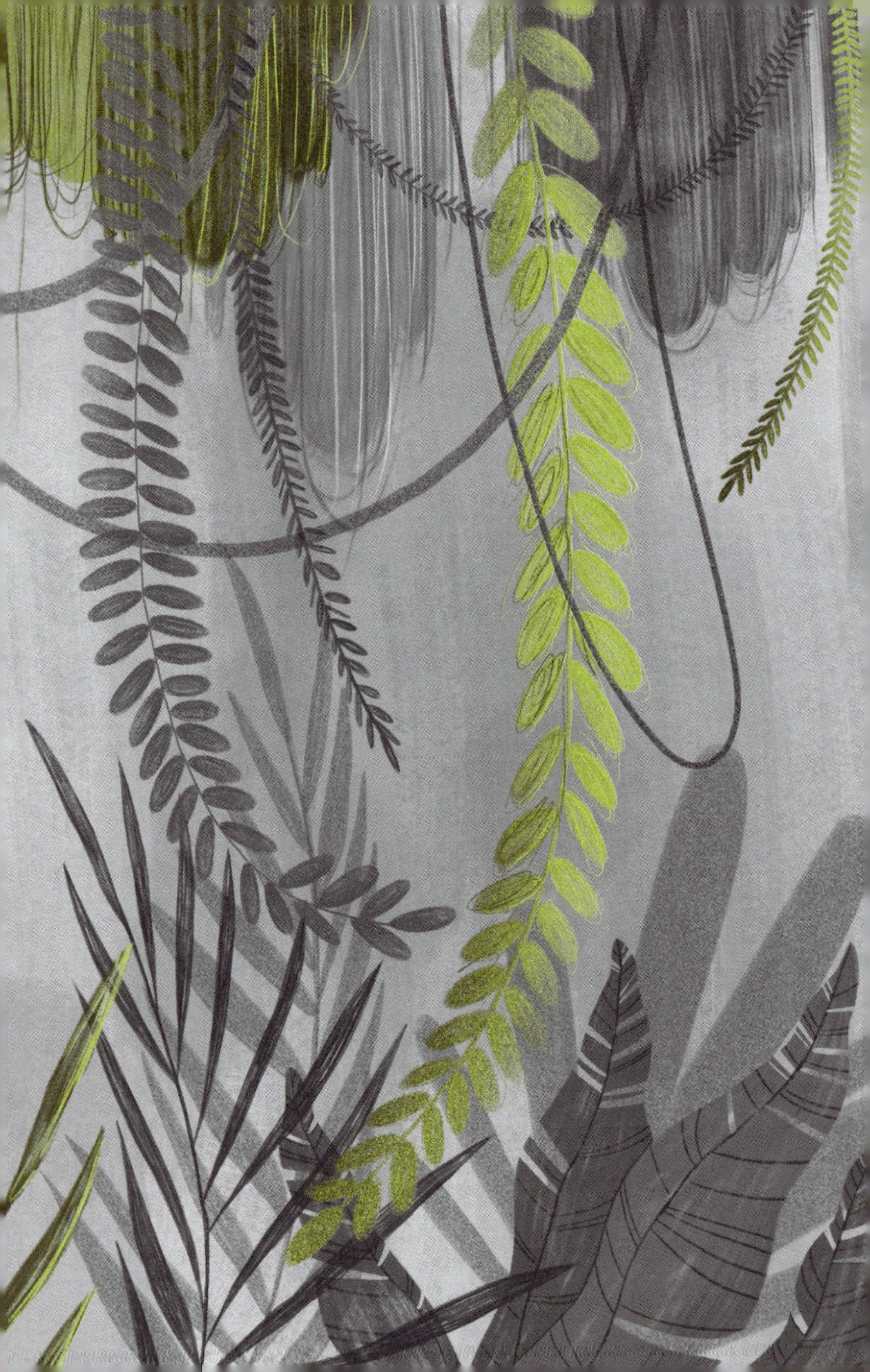

Read this book if ...

you've ever kept a

SECRET

or love the amazing

POWER OF NATURE!

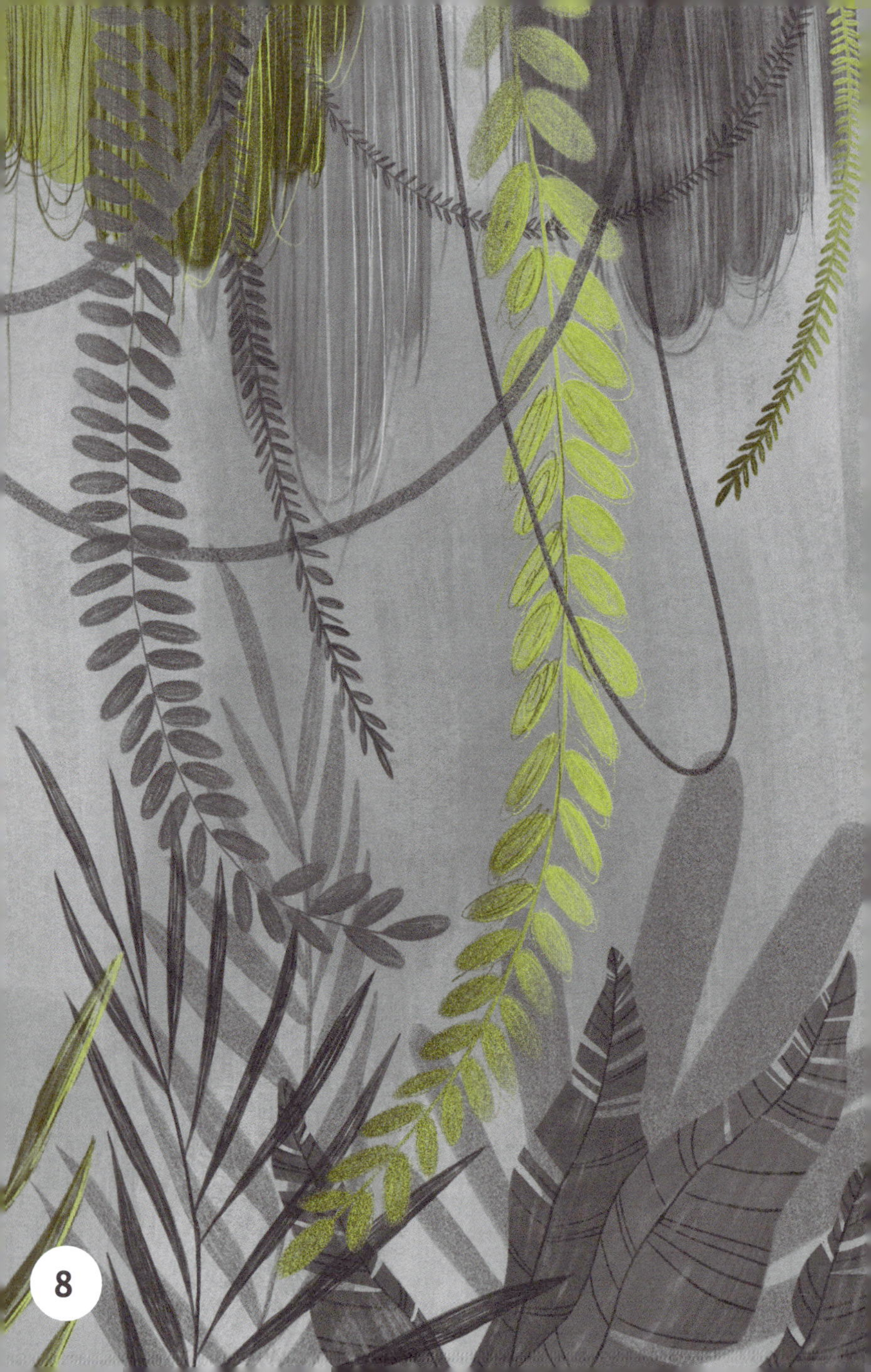

STOP AND THINK

In this book, Tala learns a very important lesson and works out who and what's important to her.

Look at the cover. What do you think this book is about? What could be in the Lake of Secrets?

Meet the characters ...

Tala

Datu

Tala's mum and dad

Sinta , the village leader

Chapter 1
The well

Once upon a time, there was a village near a hot, steamy jungle. The village was home to a girl called Tala and her family.

'Never go into that jungle alone,' Tala's mother warned her. 'Promise me, my *little sparrow*.'

Tala rolled her eyes. 'I know, Mum,' she replied. 'You tell me every day. **Please** stop calling me sparrow. I'm nearly grown up!'

'Tiny-winy sparrow!'

mocked Datu, Tala's brother.
Being mean was just his style.
He continued to tease her all day.

'Tala is a **tiny-lickle-winy-ickle** sparrow!' Datu said.

Then he roared with laughter.

'Datu NEVER gets told off, just because he's the youngest. **It's not fair!**' Tala thought. She scowled at Datu.

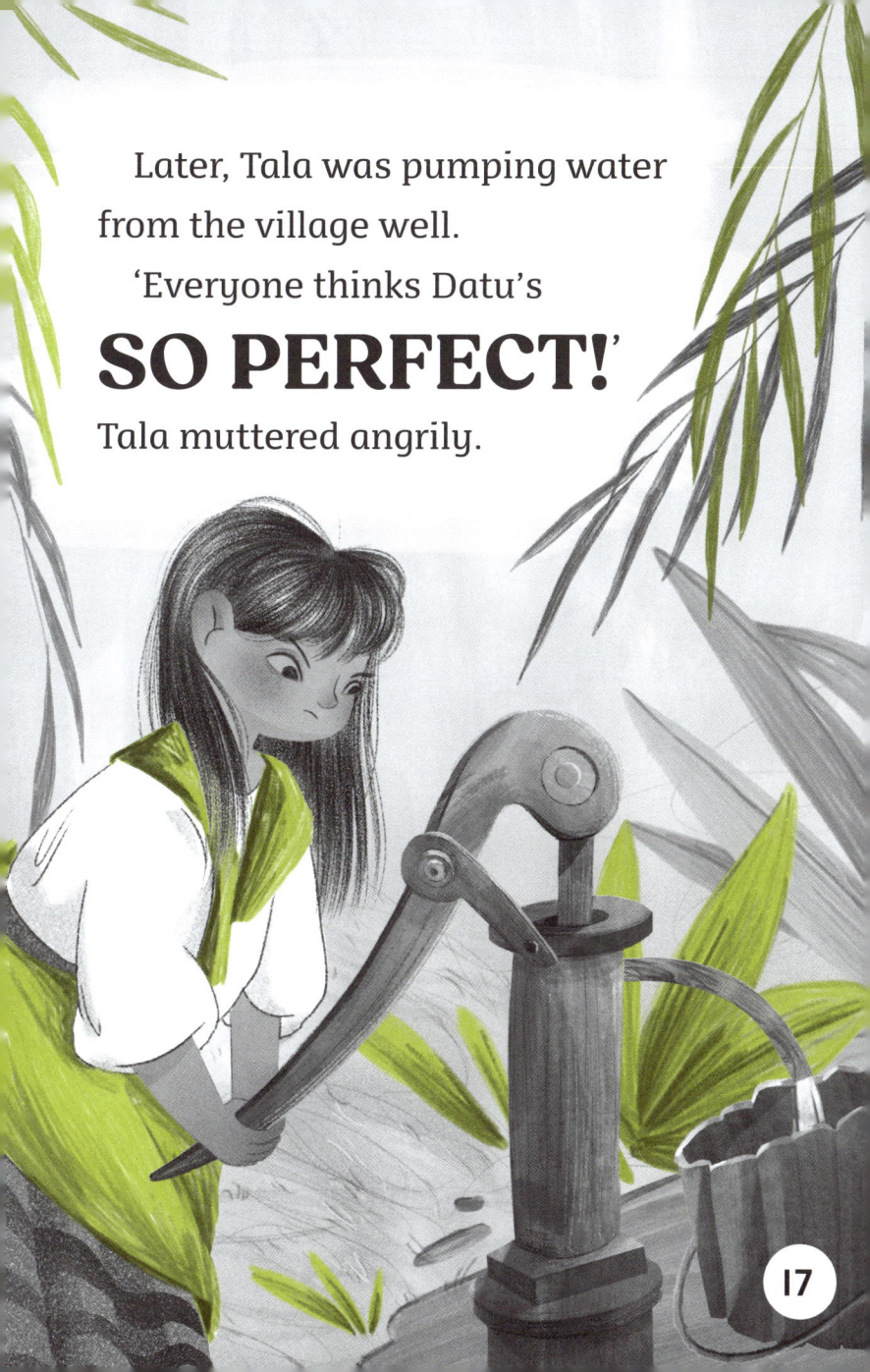

Later, Tala was pumping water from the village well.

'Everyone thinks Datu's **SO PERFECT!**' Tala muttered angrily.

A thought crossed Tala's mind. It wasn't a nice thought. It was a **dark**, **bad** thought. Yet it sent a *fizz of excitement* down her neck.

Tala *rushed* home to find some tools and something of Datu's.

Early the next morning, a loud cry woke the sleepy village.

Oh!

Everyone *rushed* to the well.
'The pump is broken,'
announced Sinta, the village leader.
'Someone has done this on purpose!'
The crowd **gasped** in shock.

Tala's father pushed to the front. He looked at the pump. 'The pipe has been **cut**,' he said. 'The handle is **broken**, too.'

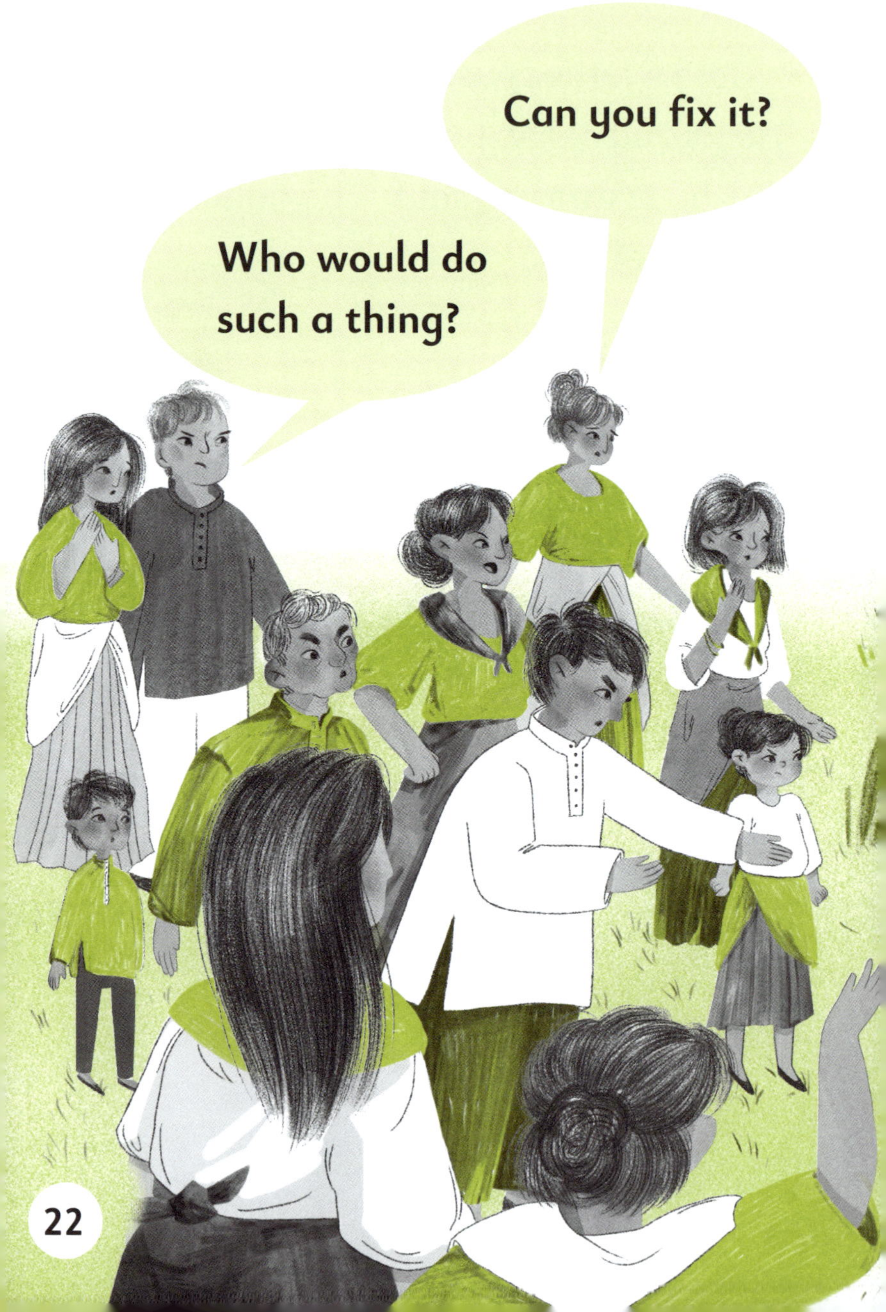
Can you fix it?
Who would do such a thing?

'I think we can fix the pump,' said Sinta. 'It will take **days** to get the parts, though.'

The crowd of villagers began to **complain loudly**.

'But we need water NOW!' someone called out.

'We must fetch water from the next village,' said Sinta.

'But it's a *long* walk!' complained another villager.

'Who is responsible for this **crime**?' another voice called out.

'**QUIET!** I see something,' shouted Tala's dad above the noise.

The crowd fell silent. Tala's dad *tugged* at something stuck in the broken handle.

'What is that?' asked Sinta.

'It looks like a piece of Datu's shirt,' said Tala's dad, frowning. **'Where's Datu?'**

Everyone looked at Datu. He was standing next to his mother and Tala. Datu looked **embarrassed**.

'This **matches** the shirt we purchased for your birthday,' Datu's mum said to him.

'Did you do this, Datu?'

M ... m ... me?

Datu's mother **gasped**.

'Datu, your clothes are torn. You *did* do this!' she said.

Datu was **shaking**. Tears filled his eyes.

Look back

1. Why is Tala annoyed with Datu?

2. How do you think Datu feels when he's accused of breaking the water pump?

3. What do you think Tala might have done?

Chapter 2
The blame

A storm arose in the night. It wasn't the ***THUNDER*** and ***LIGHTNING*** that kept Tala awake, though.

Tala's chest felt tight. It was like a JUNGLE VINE was wrapped around it.

She squeezed her eyes shut. She could still see Datu's tearful face, though.

'He deserved it!' Tala told herself. Then she **moaned**. 'Of course he didn't,' she thought. 'I should tell Mum and Dad **right now** ...

I really should ...

but maybe tomorrow.'

In the morning, things got **worse**.

'Your brother says someone else broke the pump,' said Dad.

'Tala, **promise us** that it wasn't **you**,' said Mum.

'Me? No!'

exclaimed Tala.

'If it was Datu, he will be **PUNISHED**,' said Dad.

'He will help me to fix the pump.'

'Datu **won't** be allowed to play with his friends until it's done,' Dad said.

Tala **gasped**. 'This is wrong,' she thought. 'I must say it was me!' She opened her mouth, but the words **stuck** in her throat. She thought she might burst into tears. Her mother hugged her.

'Little sparrow, don't cry. This is **not your fault.** Datu must learn his lesson,' said Tala's mother.

That evening, Sinta, the village leader, sat under the great **BANYAN TREE**. Her eyes were closed.

Tala wandered past. She was kicking at the dirt.

'I recognize that look, girl,' said Sinta.

'What do you mean?' Tala replied in surprise.

'There's a **secret** inside you. It needs to get out,' said Sinta.

'I'm not hiding anything,' said Tala hurriedly. However, her quick reply hinted she was lying.

'If you say so,' said Sinta.

'You know, I have a **secret**, too,' said Sinta. 'Come closer. I will tell you. It may help.'

Tala put her ear close to Sinta's wrinkly face. Tala listened to her in **amazement**.

Look back

1. What was stopping Tala from sleeping?

2. Why do you think Tala didn't tell the truth when she was asked?

3. Can you find four verbs in the past tense and two in the future tense in Chapter 2?

Chapter 3
The Jungle of Whispers

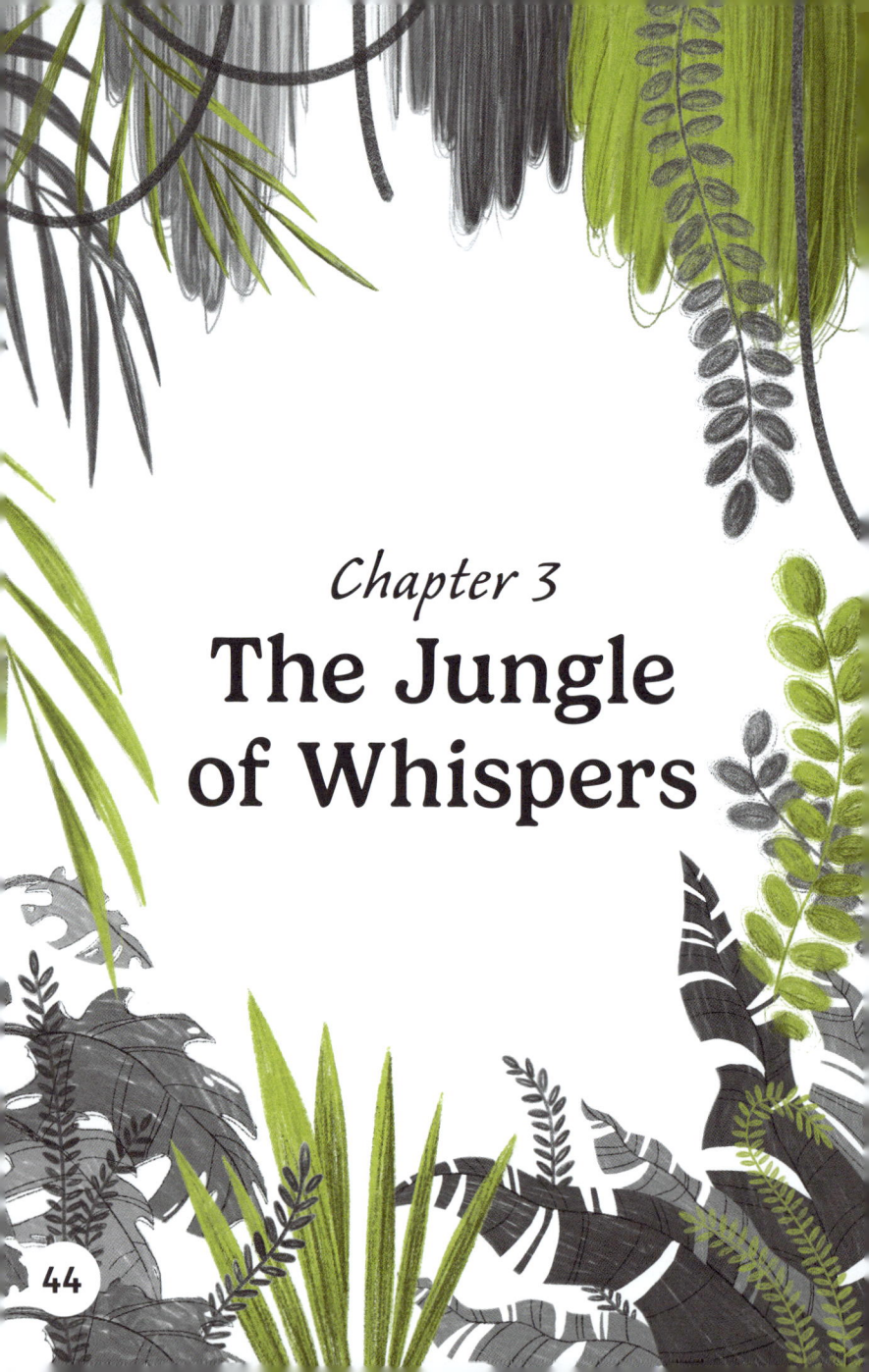

Tala stood in front of a thick wall of **TOWERING TREES** and **CLINGY CREEPERS**. She thought about what Sinta had told her.

'Enter the forest,' the village leader had said. 'You must do this **alone**.'

However, Tala kept thinking about what Mum had told her.

'Never go into that jungle alone!' Mum had always said.

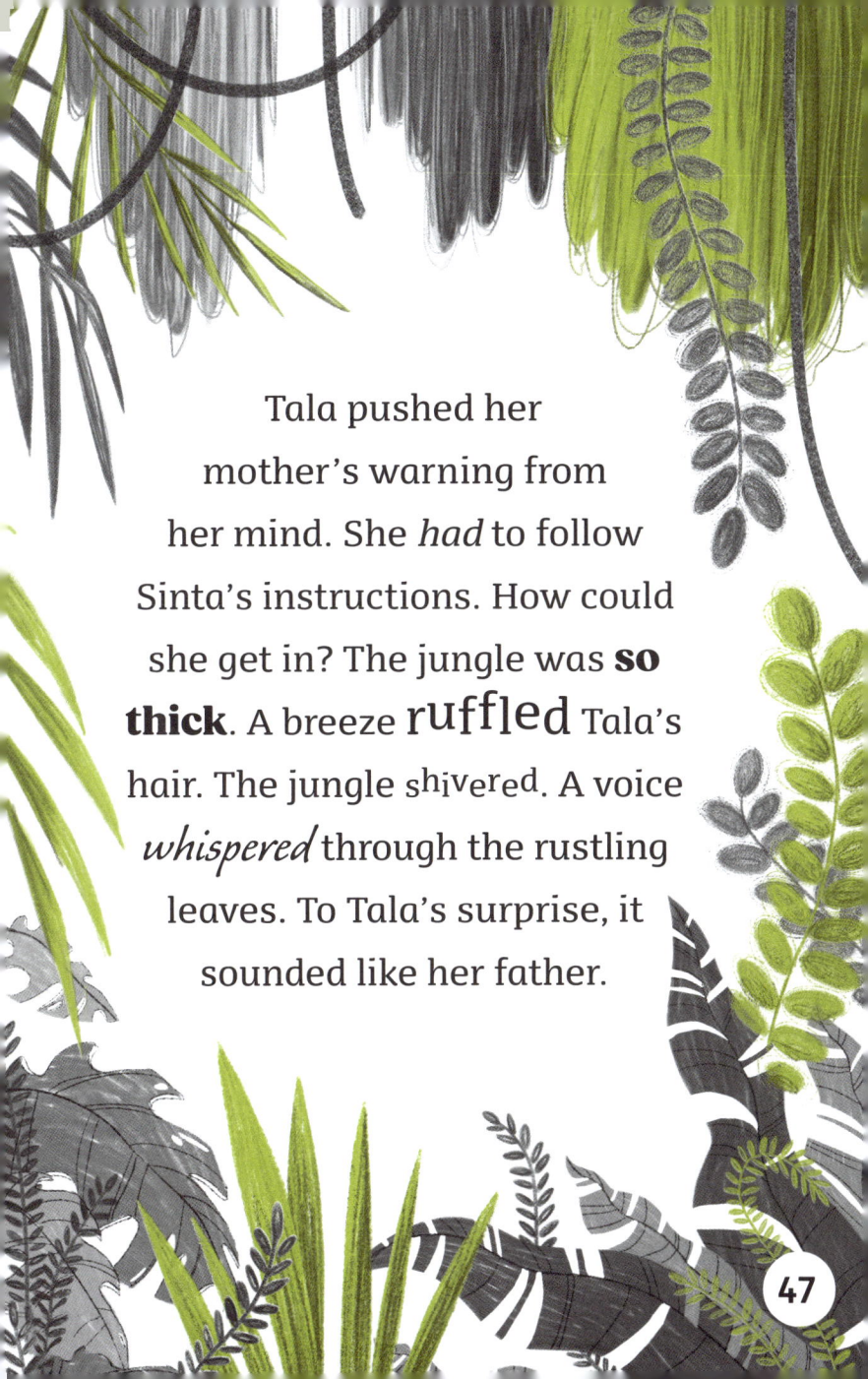

Tala pushed her mother's warning from her mind. She *had* to follow Sinta's instructions. How could she get in? The jungle was **so thick**. A breeze ruffled Tala's hair. The jungle shivered. A voice *whispered* through the rustling leaves. To Tala's surprise, it sounded like her father.

'What did you do, Tala?'

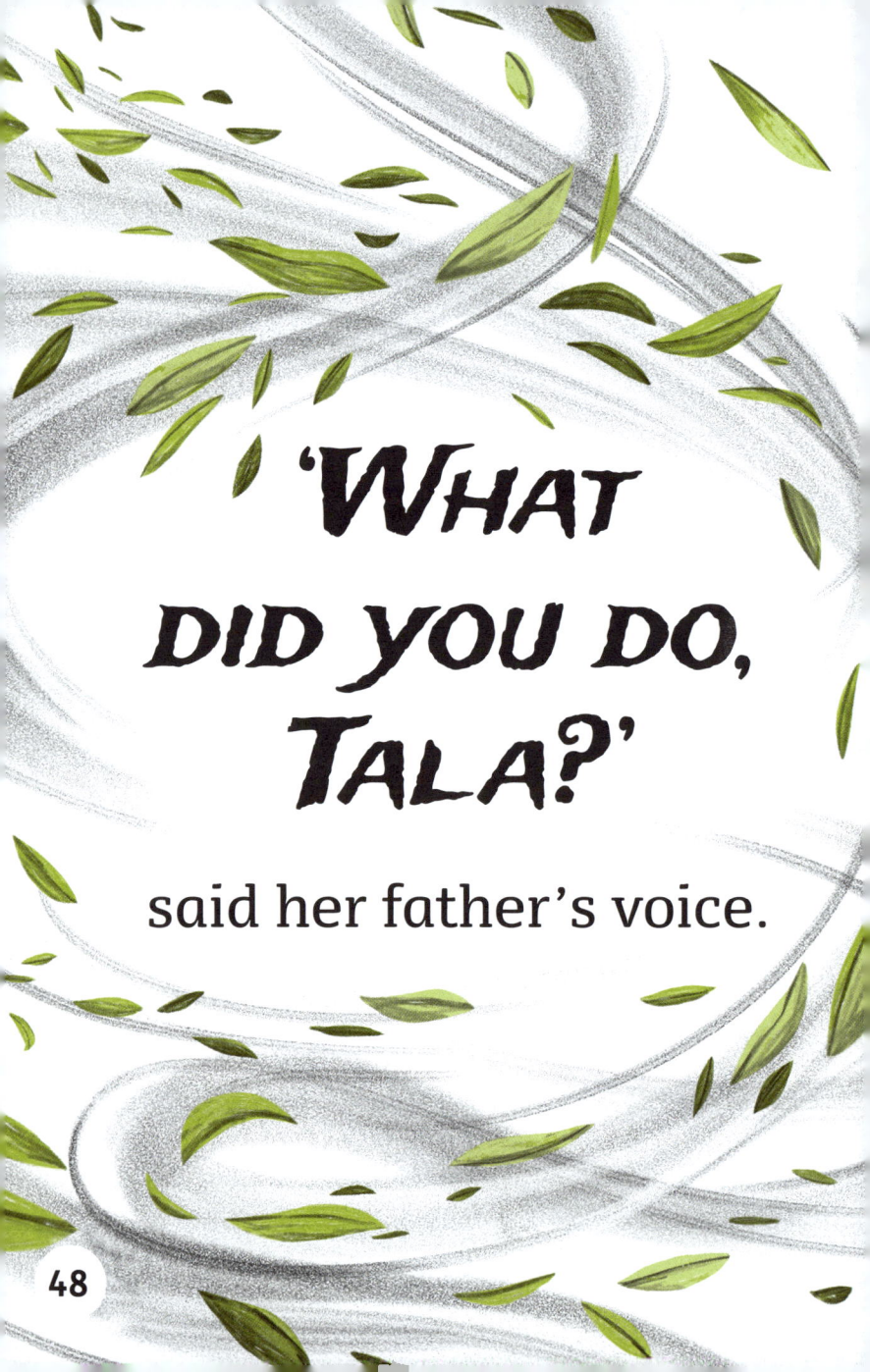

said her father's voice.

Tala gulped. 'Nothing,' she lied. Suddenly, a **POWERFUL** wind whipped around Tala. The forest **groaned**. The wind **RIPPED** green leaves from their branches.

The leaves swirled around Tala.
Then they scattered on the ground.
The green leaves had turned **dry**
and **brown** and **crinkled**.

The wind dropped. Tala noticed
a break in the green wall where the
leaves had been ripped away.

Tala remembered part of the **secret** Sinta had told her.

'Answer the whispers and choose your path,'

the village leader had said.

Tala looked around. There were **no other ways** into the jungle. 'This must be the way,' she thought.

She stepped through the break into the **hot**, **dark jungle**.

Tala followed a path through the jungle. It twisted between **DANGLING VINES** and **PRICKLY PLANTS**. All around her were the croaks and cries of hidden animals.

More of Sinta's words came back to Tala.

'Find the lake,' Sinta had said. '*Whisper* your secret into a bag of pebbles. Throw the bag into the lake and sink the secret **forever**.'

'The lake can't be much further,' Tala thought. She felt her pocket. The bag of pebbles was tucked safely inside.

The path came to a dead end. **SPIKY BRANCHES** blocked her way.

A welcome breeze lifted Tala's sticky hair from her face.

The jungle *whispered* again. This time it sounded like Datu.

'**Why didn't you say anything?**' said Datu's voice.

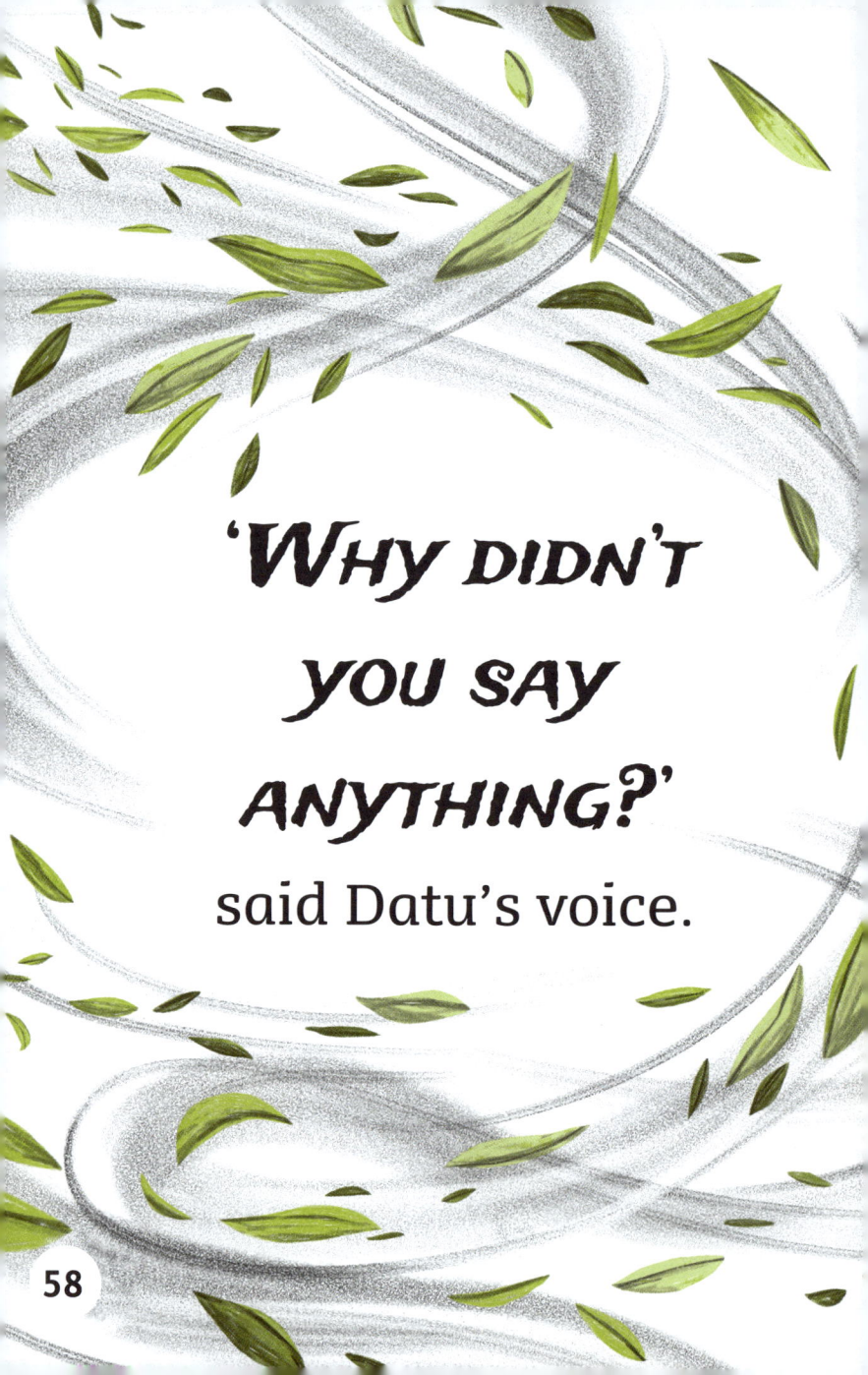

'**I TRIED!**' protested Tala. 'I was going to, but Mum stopped me.'

A blast of air **RIPPED** through the jungle.

The **SPIKY BRANCHES** groaned and snapped. Tala covered her head as they **crashed down** around her. Then the wind dropped. Tala looked up and **gasped**.

Look back

1. Why shouldn't Tala have gone into the jungle?

2. In your own words, explain what Sinta told Tala to do in the jungle.

3. Why do you think Tala heard her dad's and brother's voices in the jungle? Think about whether the voices might be real or imaginary.

Chapter 4
The Lake of Secrets

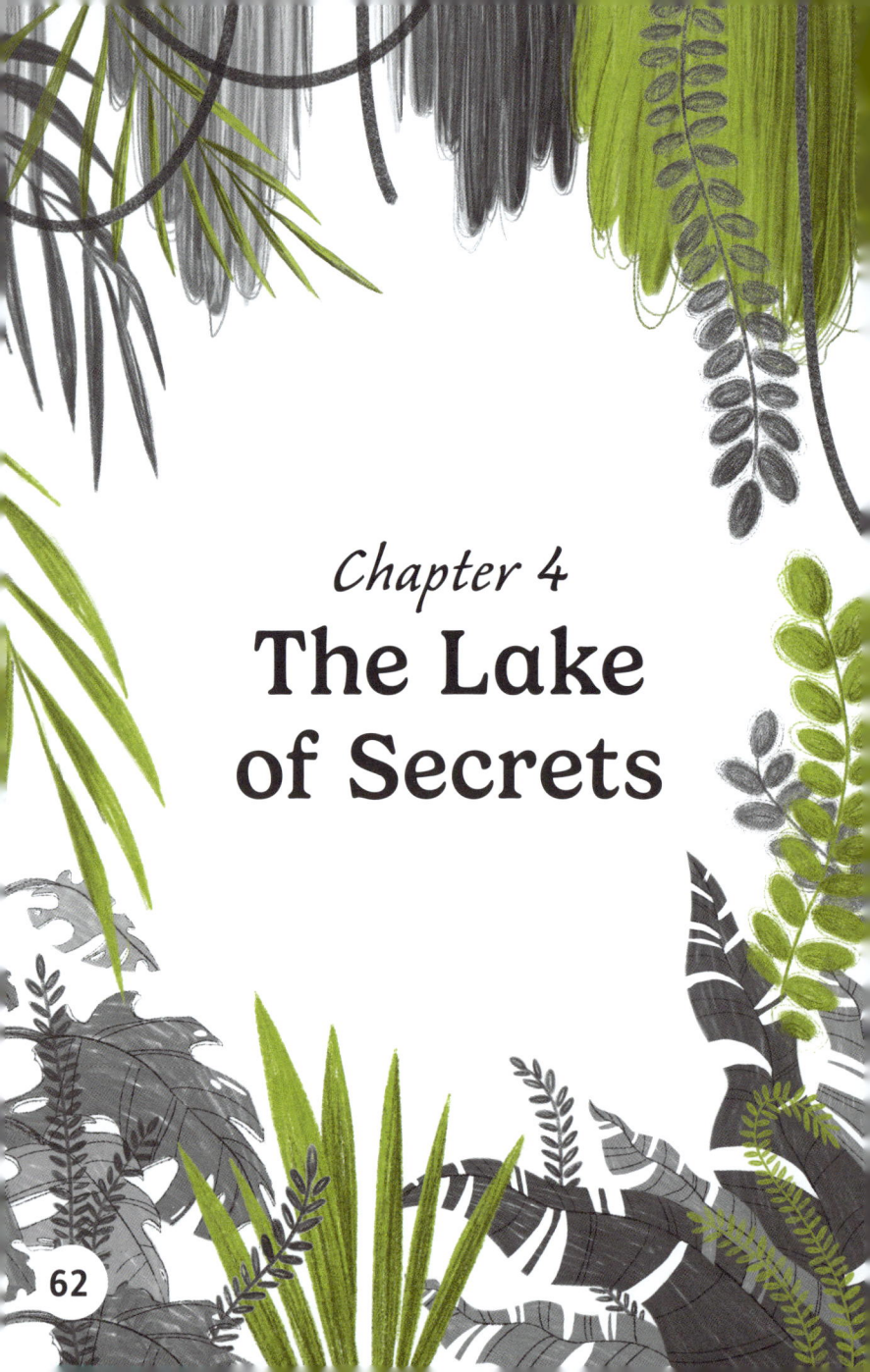

The wind had **R!PPED** a large, ugly hole through the trees. Tala spotted something attractive glistening in the distance. Water!

Tala picked her way through the tattered leaves and splintered wood.

She saw a perfectly round clearing. In the centre was a perfectly round lake.

Tala soaked up the sunshine by the lake. She **didn't notice** that the jungle animals were *silent*.

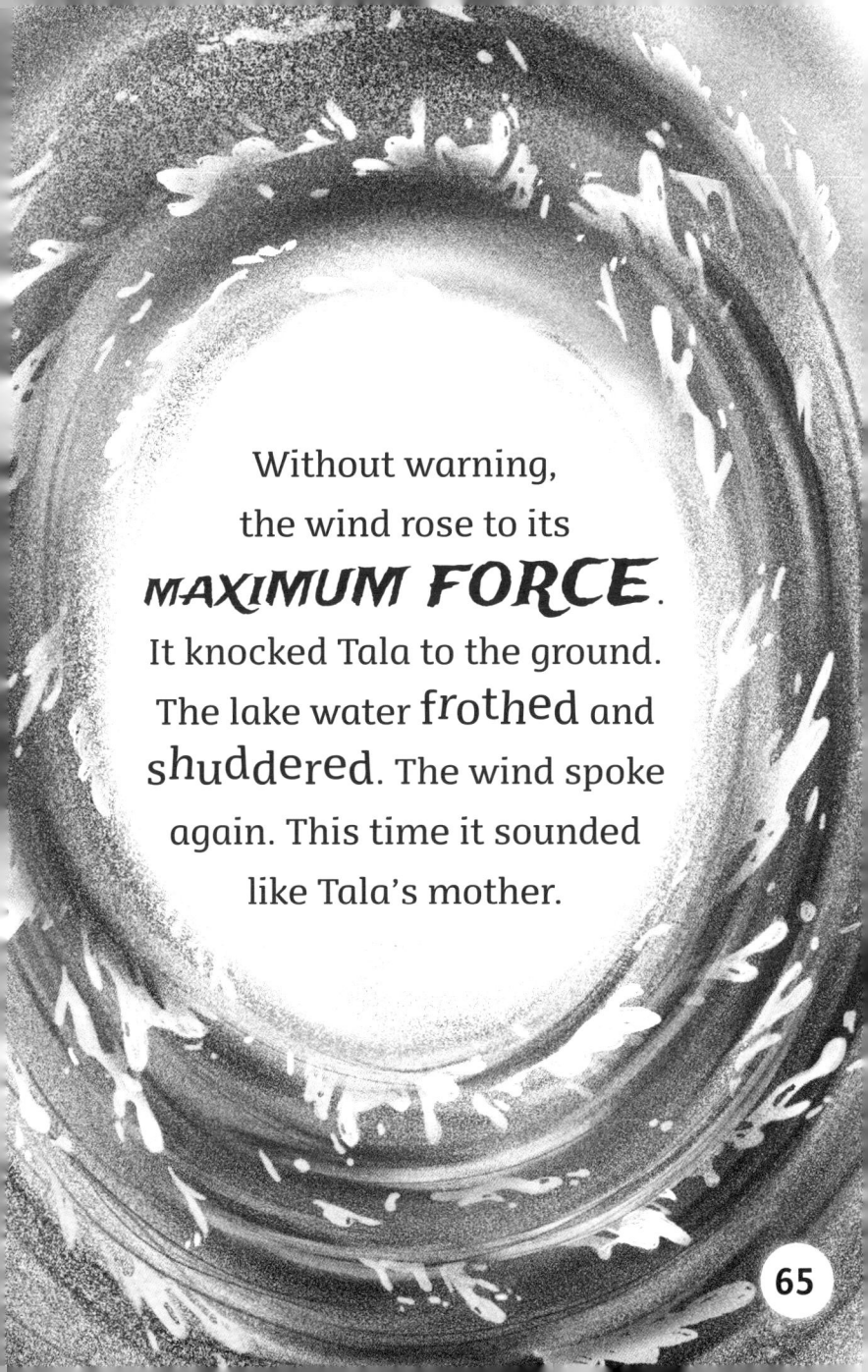

Without warning,
the wind rose to its
MAXIMUM FORCE.
It knocked Tala to the ground.
The lake water frothed and
shuddered. The wind spoke
again. This time it sounded
like Tala's mother.

'Who is to blame, Tala?'

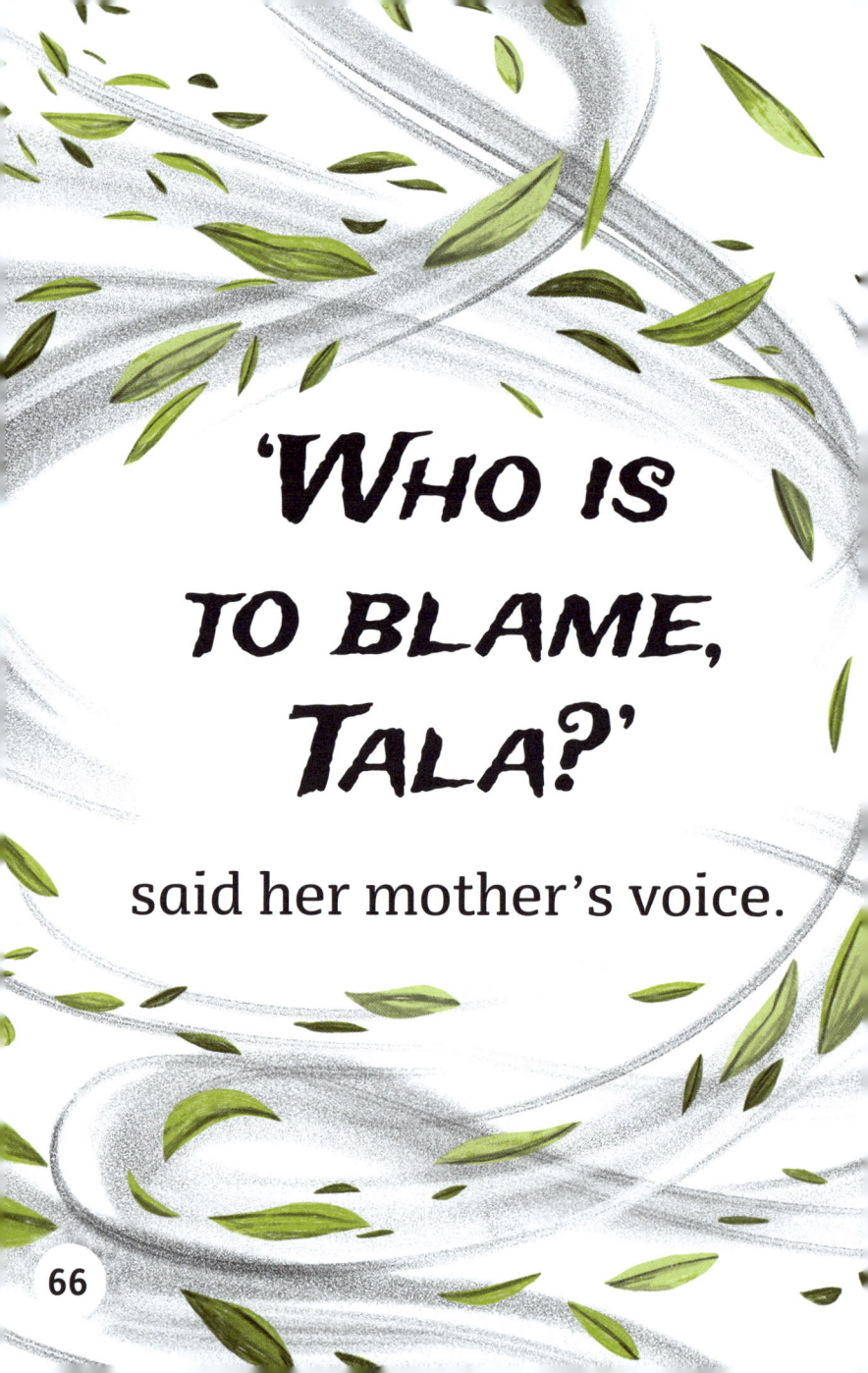

said her mother's voice.

'It wasn't my fault!'

protested Tala.

Tala slowly lifted her head and watched in **HORROR** as the water drained out of the lake. It was like bathwater gurgling down a plughole.

'**NO!**' Tala shouted, but the lake was gone.

Tala squelched out onto the huge circle of mud.

She **slipped** and **slid** until she reached a tiny puddle.

Tala pulled the bag of pebbles from her pocket. She opened the bag.

'*I broke the pump and blamed my brother*,' Tala whispered. 'Lake of Secrets, take my **secret** … and hide it forever.'

Tala threw the bag into the puddle. It sank a little, but still **stuck out**. Tala crawled forward. She **pressed** the bag into the muddy water, but it wouldn't stay under.

'Please!' Tala begged.

The wind ROARED again.

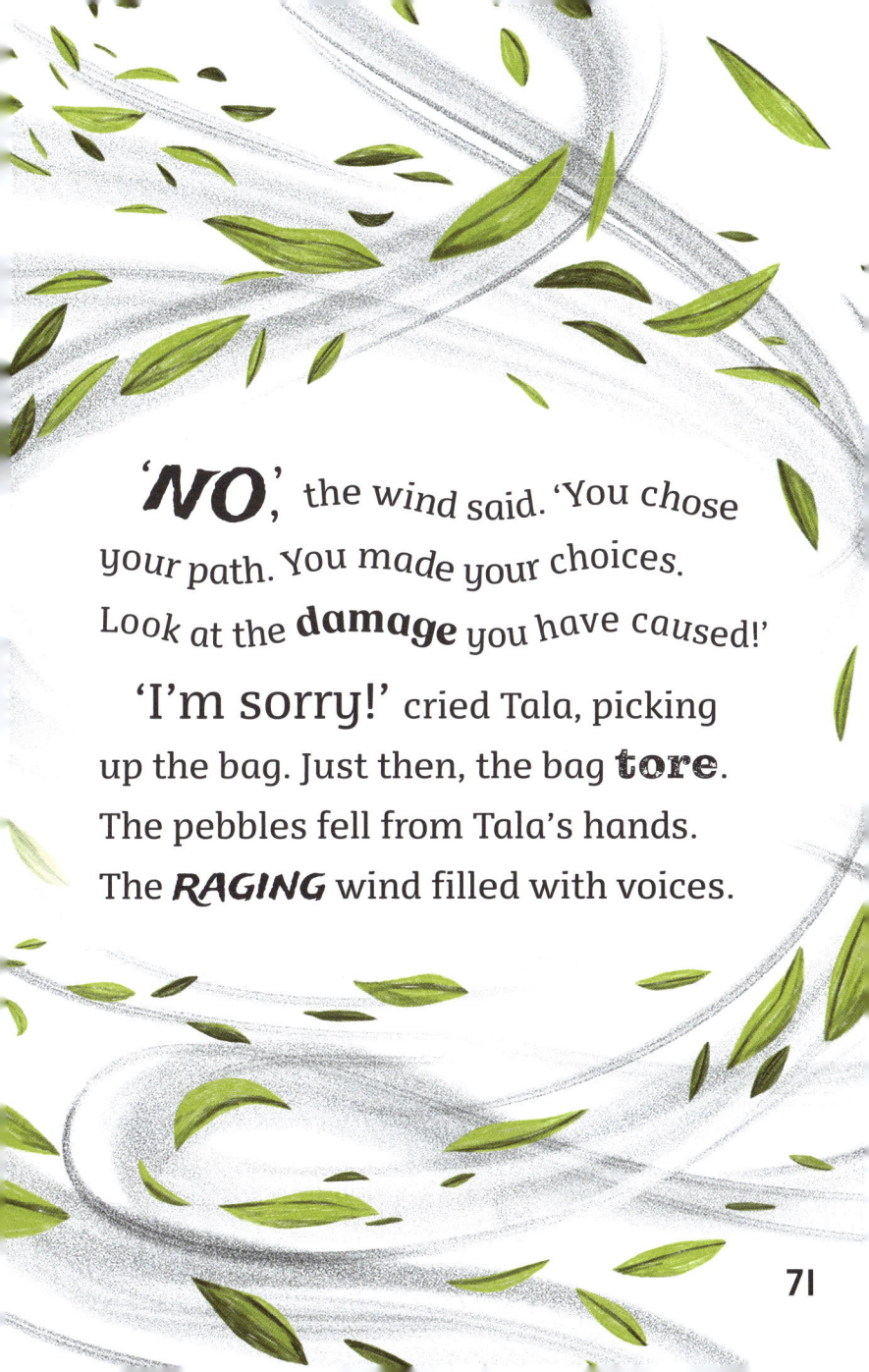

'**NO**', the wind said. 'You chose your path. You made your choices. Look at the **damage** you have caused!'

'I'm sorry!' cried Tala, picking up the bag. Just then, the bag **tore**. The pebbles fell from Tala's hands. The **RAGING** wind filled with voices.

Oh, the liar!

The truth is out!

SHAMEFUL!

SHE BLAMED HER BROTHER!

HOW COULD SHE?

Tala covered her ears.
She caught sight of her own
reflection in the puddle.

'It's not too late. Tell the truth,'

the wind roared. This time it sounded like Sinta's voice.

'I will tell the truth! I will!' Tala said.

The voices dropped to a whisper. '*Go home and heal your family*,' they said.

As Tala *rushed* home, the lake slowly filled. The jungle healed behind her.

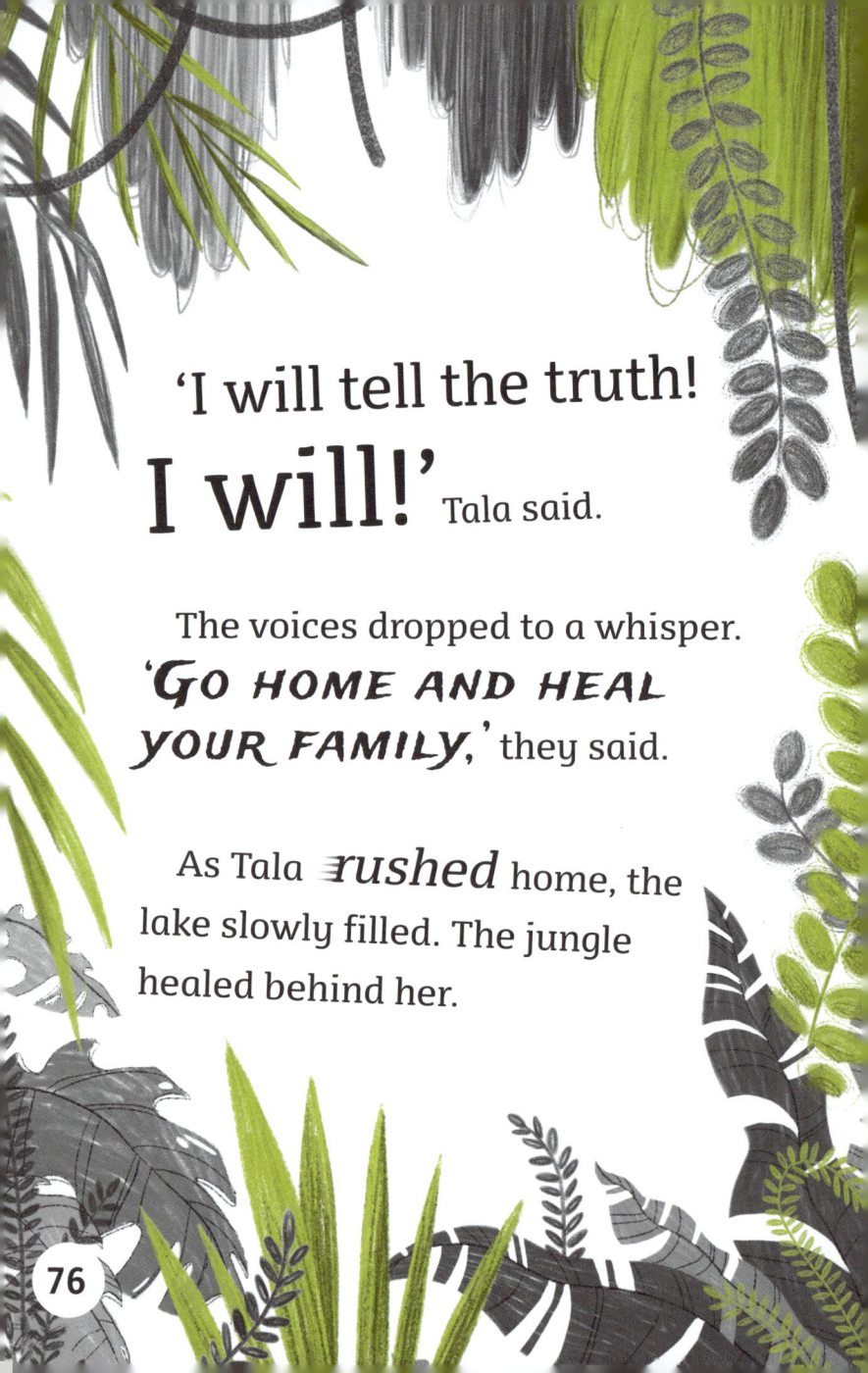

Look back

1. What has Tala learned from her visit to the lake?
2. What do you think will happen when Tala returns home?
3. Describe Tala's feelings when the water drained away.

Chapter 5
The truth

'Tala! My poor girl, what happened to you?' asked Tala's mother.

Tala was standing by the well. Her clothes were **ripped** and covered in mud.

'Let's get you home, little sparrow,' said Mum.

'NO!' Tala replied firmly.
'I have something to say.

To you, to Dad, to Datu, and everyone in the village.'

Tala took a deep breath.

She told the truth.

A few days later, Tala was sitting under the banyan tree with Sinta.

Some villagers walked past. They **glared** at Tala and shook their heads. Tala **sighed**.

'They will **forgive** you in time,' said Sinta. 'So will your parents and Datu, eventually.'

'I hope so,' said Tala.

'Heal your family with *love* and *kindness*,' Sinta replied.

'Did you know what would happen at the lake?' Tala asked.

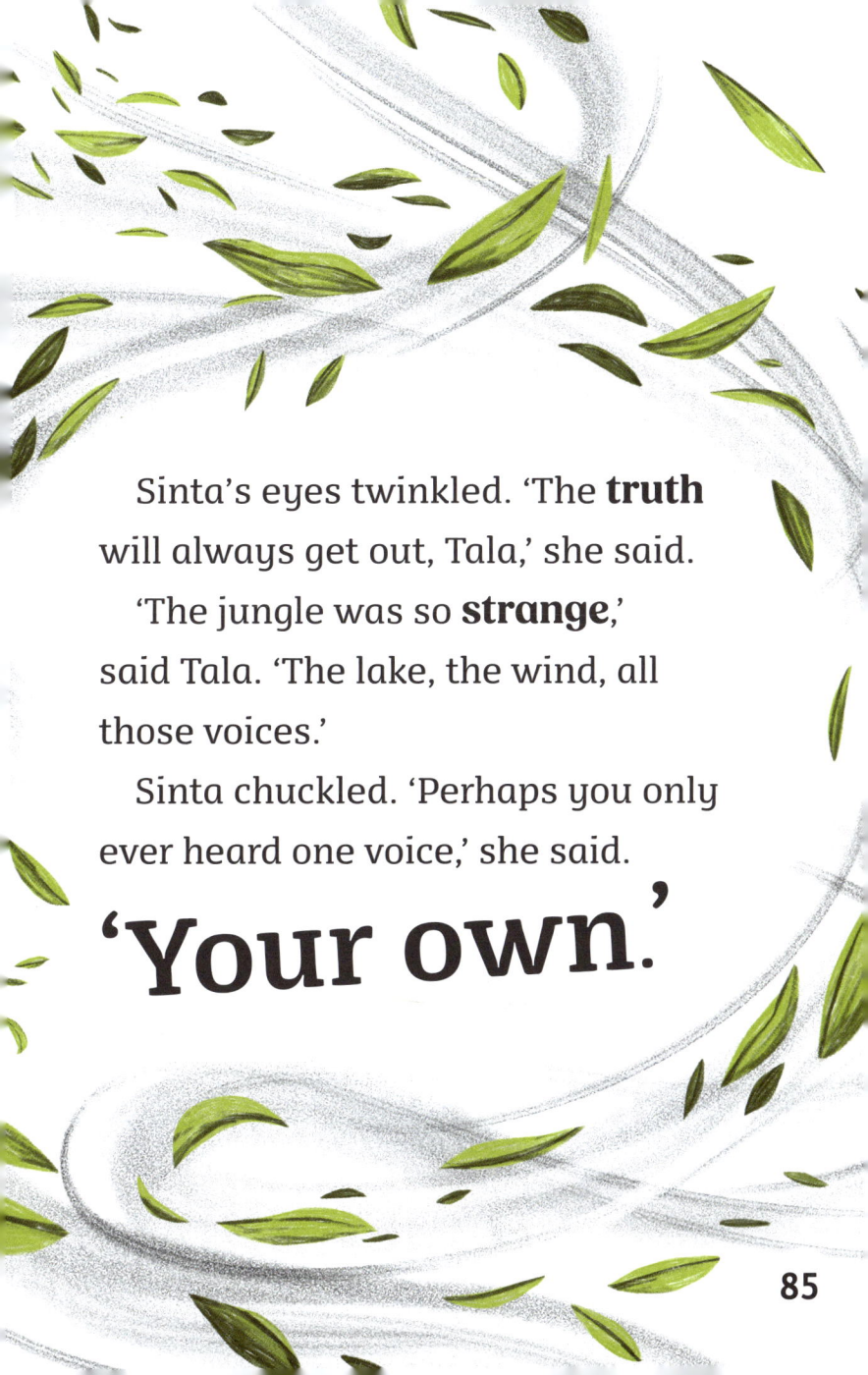

Sinta's eyes twinkled. 'The **truth** will always get out, Tala,' she said.

'The jungle was so **strange**,' said Tala. 'The lake, the wind, all those voices.'

Sinta chuckled. 'Perhaps you only ever heard one voice,' she said.

'Your own.'

Look back

1. Have you ever let anyone else take the blame for something you've done? How did you feel? Did the truth come out in the end?

2. Why do you think Tala heard so many different voices when she was by the lake?

3. What lessons can you learn from this story?

HA! HA!

How did Tala feel when she entered the jungle?

She couldn't be-leaf her eyes!

Read out loud

Here is a poem called *Tala's Lesson*. It's about the story you've just read.

Read the poem in your head and think about the meaning of each sentence. Think about how you could say each line to express its meaning. Are there any actions you could add?

Practise saying the poem out loud before you perform it.

poem

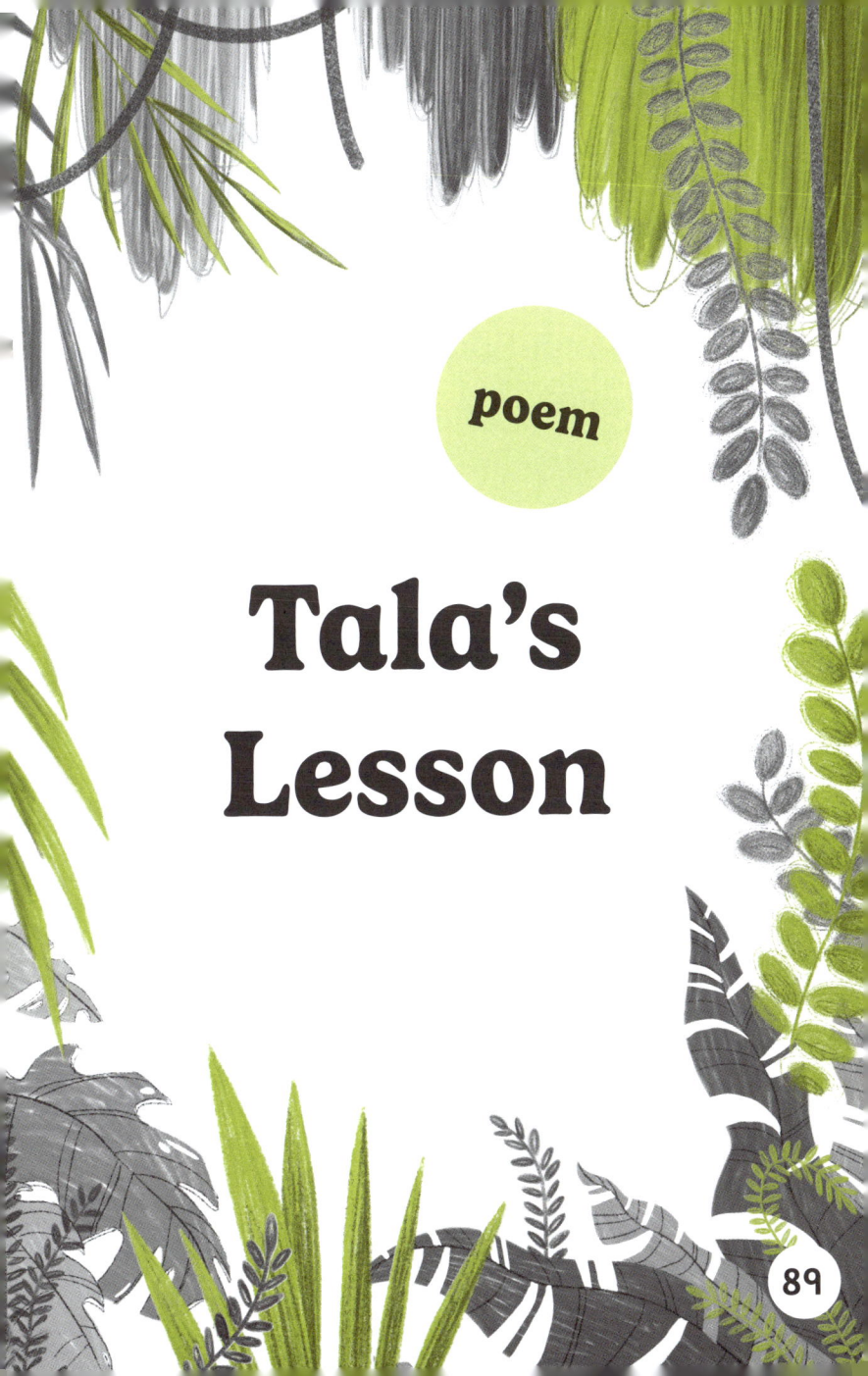

Tala's Lesson

Tala was a girl who was jealous of her brother,
So she broke the village pump and put him in some bother.
Tala couldn't sleep but she wouldn't confess,
She let Datu take the blame and all the distress.
Her mum and dad were sad and Tala felt bad,
She had hurt the only brother that she had ever had.

Tala made her way to a special
   jungle lake,
Where the water taught her that it's
   never too late.
You can tell the truth and admit you
   were wrong,
Say sorry to your family and try to
   get along.

Read it again

1. Perform the poem to a friend or family member. What did you think of your performance? What could you do differently?

2. Try memorizing the poem. Then try performing it again without using the book.

3. Can you come up with some more lines to add to the end of the poem? Think about what might have happened after the story finished. Perhaps Datu forgave Tala, or he apologized for laughing at her.